Sometimes strange things happen, and nobody can explain why. A door opens in the night, but there is nobody there. A cold hand takes you by the neck, but you are alone, and it is a warm day. You go into a house, and it is full of people. You cannot see them, but you can feel them there, waiting in the dark.

Rhoda is a farm worker. She is tall, with beautiful dark eyes, and works long hours for not much money. Gertrude does not work. She is pretty, has small white hands, a sweet smile, and beautiful dresses. Mr Lodge is a farmer, with a big farmhouse, and many fine cows on his rich farm. Which of the two women is the wife of Farmer Lodge? Which woman did he love, which woman does he love, which woman is the mother of his son?

And which of these people has a withered arm? A poor, thin, withered arm, an arm with the marks of fingers on it, an arm that grows thinner and more withered, week by week. How did those marks get there? Nobody knows, nobody can explain them. But people say they are a witch's marks . . .

OXFORD BOOKWORMS LIBRARY
Classics

The Withered Arm

Stage 1 (400 headwords)

Series Editor: Jennifer Bassett
Founder Editor: Tricia Hedge
Activities Editors: Jennifer Bassett and Christine Lindop

THOMAS HARDY

The Withered Arm

Retold by
Jennifer Bassett

Illustrated by
Bob Harvey

OXFORD UNIVERSITY PRESS

OXFORD
UNIVERSITY PRESS

Great Clarendon Street, Oxford OX2 6DP

Oxford University Press is a department of the University of Oxford.
It furthers the University's objective of excellence in research, scholarship,
and education by publishing worldwide in

Oxford New York

Auckland Cape Town Dar es Salaam Hong Kong Karachi
Kuala Lumpur Madrid Melbourne Mexico City Nairobi
New Delhi Shanghai Taipei Toronto

With offices in

Argentina Austria Brazil Chile Czech Republic France Greece
Guatemala Hungary Italy Japan Poland Portugal Singapore
South Korea Switzerland Thailand Turkey Ukraine Vietnam

OXFORD and OXFORD ENGLISH are registered trade marks of
Oxford University Press in the UK and in certain other countries

ISBN 978 0 19 478925 7

A complete recording of this Bookworms edition of
The Withered Arm is available on audio CD ISBN 978 0 19 478860 1

Printed in Hong Kong

Word count (main text): 5735 words

For more information on the Oxford Bookworms Library,
visit www.oup.com/elt/bookworms

CONTENTS

The milkmaid and the wife

It was six o'clock on a warm April evening, milking time for Farmer Lodge's eighty cows. They stood quietly in the dairy, and the milkmaids were all at work.

'They say Farmer Lodge is coming home with his new wife tomorrow,' said one milkmaid.

'Yes. And she's young and pretty, I hear,' a second girl said.

She looked past her cow to the other end of the dairy. There was another milkmaid there, a thin, older woman, about thirty years old.

The first girl looked at the older woman too. 'I'm sorry for *her*,' she said quietly to her friend.

'Oh no,' said the second girl. 'That was years and years ago. Farmer Lodge never speaks to Rhoda Brook these days.'

When the milking was finished, the milkmaids left the dairy and went home. The thin woman, Rhoda Brook, did not walk to the village with the other girls. She went up the hill behind the farm to a little house near the trees. It was a poor house, of only two rooms, and the roof did not keep the rain out.

'I'm sorry for her,' the milkmaid said to her friend.

At the door of the house the woman met her son, a boy of about twelve, and they went inside.

'I heard something at the dairy today,' the woman said. 'Your father is bringing his young wife home tomorrow. I want you to go and look at her.'

'Yes, mother,' said the boy. 'Is father married then?'

'Yes . . . You can go into town and do my shopping for me. And when you see her, there or on the road, look at her carefully.'

'Yes, mother.'

'What is she like? I want to know. Is she tall, is she short? Are her eyes blue or brown or green? Look at the colour of her hair, the colour of her dress. And look at her hands. Does she have small white hands, or the hands of a milkmaid, a worker's hands? You must look at all these things, and tell me.'

'Yes, mother,' the boy said again. He took a piece of bread from the table and began to eat it.

His mother said nothing more, but turned her thin, pale face to the open door. Her beautiful dark eyes stared out at the trees, seeing and not seeing.

🐝 🐝 🐝

The next evening was warm and sunny. The road from the town to the farm went up and down a number of hills, and near the top of one big hill the boy saw a carriage behind him. It was Farmer Lodge with his new wife. She was a pretty young thing, much younger than her husband, with a sweet, innocent face.

The boy carried a heavy bag, and was happy to stop and stare for a minute. The carriage came slowly up the hill, and the boy took a good long look at the farmer's wife. His eyes never left her face.

3

The farmer did not look at the boy once, and at the top of the hill the carriage went faster, leaving the boy behind.

'How that poor boy stared at me!' said the young wife.

'Yes, my love. I saw that,' the farmer said.

'Is he a boy from the village?'

The boy took a good long look at the farmer's wife.

'No. I think he lives with his mother on one of these hills.'

'He knows you, then.'

'Of course. And everyone is going to stare at you at first, my pretty Gertrude.'

'Yes, I know. But that poor boy had a very heavy bag. Perhaps he wanted us to help him with the bag.'

'Oh, these country boys can carry anything,' said her husband. 'They do it all the time.'

The carriage went quickly on. After a time the boy left the road and went up the hill to his mother's house.

She was home before him. She took the heavy bag from him and began to take the things out.

'Well, did you see her?'

'Yes. I had a good look at her on the road.'

'And what is she like?'

'She's nice.'

'Is she young?'

'Well, she's older than me.'

'Of course she is. But is she older than *me*?'

'No, she's younger.'

'Ah. What colour is her hair?'

'It's a brown colour, and her face is very pretty.'

'Are her eyes dark?'

'No, they're blue, and her mouth is very nice and red, and when she smiles, you can see white teeth.'

'Is she tall?' said the woman, a little angrily.

'I couldn't see. She was in the carriage.'

'Then tomorrow you must go to church. Go early, before she and Mr Lodge arrive, and watch her when she walks in. Then come home and tell me.'

'Very well, mother. But why don't *you* go and look at her?'

'Never! I don't want to see her. She was with Mr Lodge, of course. Did he look at you or speak to you?'

'No.'

The next day the boy went to church, and waited and watched. When Mr and Mrs Lodge arrived, everybody – not just the boy – stared at the new wife with interest.

When the boy reached home, his mother said, 'Well?'

'She's not tall. She's short,' the boy said.

'Ah!' said his mother, pleased.

'But she's very pretty – very. She had a beautiful white dress on, and it made a lot of noise when she moved. Mr Lodge looked very happy with her.'

'No more now,' said the woman. 'You can tell me more later.'

In the next days, Rhoda Brook heard more and more from her son about the new wife. The boy often saw Mrs Lodge around the farmhouse, but his mother never saw her, and never went near the farmhouse.

At the dairy the other milkmaids talked a lot about

'Mr Lodge looked very happy with her,' the boy said.

the new wife. They usually stopped when Rhoda was near, but she heard some of it. She remembered everything, and forgot nothing.

And slowly Rhoda Brook made a picture in her head of the young Mrs Lodge – a picture as good, as true as a photograph.

2

The dream

One night, two or three weeks later, when the boy was in bed, Rhoda Brook sat by the dying fire in her little house. She stared at the fire for a long time, but she saw only the picture in her head of the new wife. At last, tired from her day's work, she went to bed.

But the picture of Gertrude Lodge did not go away. When Rhoda slept, the young wife was still there in Rhoda's dreams. She sat on Rhoda's body in the bed, staring into Rhoda's face. Her blue eyes were cold, and with a cruel laugh, she put her left hand in front of Rhoda's eyes. There, on the third finger, was her wedding-ring. And the phantom of Gertrude Lodge laughed again.

Rhoda turned this way and that way, but the phantom was still there. It sat, heavier and heavier, on Rhoda's body, and now Rhoda could not move. Always in her ears was that cruel laugh, and always in front of her eyes was that left hand with its wedding-ring.

At last, half-dead with terror, Rhoda suddenly put out her right hand, took hold of the phantom's left arm, and pulled it hard.

The phantom fell off the bed onto the floor, and Rhoda sat up.

'Dear God!' she cried. She felt cold, so cold. 'That was not a dream – she was here!'

Always in her ears was that cruel laugh, and always in front of her eyes was that left hand with its wedding-ring.

She could still feel the young woman's arm under her hand – a warm, living arm. She looked on the floor for the woman's body, but there was nothing there.

Rhoda Brook slept no more that night, and at the dairy early the next morning, she looked pale and ill. She could not forget the feel of that arm under her hand.

When she came home for breakfast, her son asked her, 'What was that noise in your room last night, mother? Did you fall off the bed?'

'Noise? What time did you hear it?'

'About two o'clock. But what was it, mother? Something fell, I heard it. Was it you?'

Rhoda did not answer, and after breakfast she began to do her work in the house. At about midday she heard something, and looked out of the window. At the bottom of the garden stood a woman – the woman from her dream. Rhoda stood still, and stared.

The boy came to look out of the window too.

'Oh, there's Mrs Lodge,' he said. 'She told me—'

'Told you?' said his mother. She looked angry. 'Why did you speak to her? I told you not to.'

'She spoke to me first. I met her in the road.'

'When was this?'

'Yesterday.'

'What did you tell her?'

'Nothing. She began to talk to me, and then she saw

my old shoes. She said, "Do they keep the rain out?" And I said, "No, they don't, but mother and I have no money for new shoes." Then she said, "I can give you some better shoes." She's bringing them now, I think. Perhaps they're in her bag. She's very nice, mother – she gives things to lots of people.'

By now Mrs Lodge was at the door. Rhoda wanted to run away, but there was no back door in her little house. So she waited, and the boy ran to open the door.

The boy ran to open the door.

'This is the right house then,' said Mrs Lodge, smiling at the boy. 'And this is your mother, is it?'

The face and body were the same as those of the phantom in Rhoda's dream, but there was nothing cruel in this face. The blue eyes were warm, and the smile was sweet and kind.

The young woman took the shoes out of her bag, and gave them to the boy. She smiled and talked in a warm and friendly way.

'How kind she is!' thought Rhoda. 'How young and sweet and innocent! Why did I have that bad dream about her? She's a friend, not an enemy.'

🕱 🕱 🕱

Two days later Mrs Lodge came again, with a new shirt for the boy, and twelve days after that she visited Rhoda a third time. The boy was out that day.

'I like walking up here on the hill,' Mrs Lodge told Rhoda. 'And your house is the only one up here.'

They talked about the weather and the village, then Mrs Lodge got up to leave. 'Are you well, Rhoda?' she asked. 'You look pale.'

'Oh, I'm always pale,' said Rhoda. 'But what about you, Mrs Lodge? Are you well?'

'Yes, I am, but . . . there is something . . . It's nothing very bad, but I don't understand it.'

She uncovered her left hand and arm. There were

'There is something . . . It's nothing very bad,
but I don't understand it,' said Mrs Lodge.

marks on the arm, yellowy-brown marks, like marks made by fingers. Rhoda stared at them.

'How did it happen?' she asked.

'I don't know,' said Mrs Lodge. 'One night, when I was in bed, I had a dream . . . and then suddenly, my arm hurt very badly. Perhaps I hit it on something in the daytime, but I don't remember it.' She laughed. 'My dear husband says it's nothing very much, and he's right, of course.'

'Yes . . . Which night was that?' said Rhoda.

Mrs Lodge thought for a moment. 'It was two weeks ago today. It was two o'clock in the night – I remember, because I heard the clock.'

It was the same night, the same hour, as Rhoda's dream of the phantom. Rhoda remembered the terror of it, and felt cold.

'How can this be?' she thought, when Mrs Lodge left. 'Did I do that? But why? She is innocent and kind – I don't want to hurt her. And how can a thing like that happen? Only witches can do things like that . . .'

3

The face in the glass

The days went past, and Rhoda Brook was afraid to meet Mrs Lodge again. She liked her, and did not want to remember the strange dream or the strange marks on the young wife's arm. But she could not stop thinking about them.

One day they met on the road from the village. They began to talk, and after a minute or two Rhoda said, 'How is your arm, Mrs Lodge? Is it better now?'

'No, it isn't. It's worse than before. Sometimes it hurts very badly.'

'What does the doctor say about it?' asked Rhoda.

'He doesn't understand it. He just says, "Put the arm in hot water for five minutes twice a day." Well, I do that, but it doesn't help.'

'Can I look at your arm?' asked Rhoda.

Once again, the younger woman uncovered her arm, and Rhoda stared at it.

The arm was thinner, and a little withered. And the marks looked more and more like marks made by fingers. Rhoda remembered her dream, and the feel of the arm under her hand – in just the same place.

'It looks like the marks of fingers,' Gertrude Lodge said. She tried to laugh. 'My husband says they are a witch's marks. A witch put her hand on my arm, he says, and it's killing the flesh.'

'No, no,' said Rhoda quickly. She felt cold and afraid. 'Don't listen to those old stories.'

The young wife's face was unhappy. 'No, but . . . you see, I think he begins to . . . to love me less, because of these marks on my arm. Men always like their wives to be pretty, don't they?'

'Some men do,' said Rhoda. 'But don't show him the arm. Cover it all the time, and then he can't see it.'

Rhoda could see the tears in her eyes.

'Ah, but he knows the marks are there.' Gertrude looked away, but Rhoda could see the tears in her eyes.

'I hope your arm is better soon, Mrs Lodge,' she said quietly.

She said goodbye and began to walk home. She felt sorry for the poor, innocent young wife, and did not want to hurt her. But she did not feel sorry for the husband. She walked home, thinking about him. 'So, Farmer Lodge,' she thought. 'You loved me once, but then you left me, and did nothing to help me. You wanted a new, younger and prettier woman for your wife. But she is not so pretty now, is she?'

🐛 🐛 🐛

The next day Rhoda walked home from the dairy after evening milking at the usual time. She was nearly at her house when she saw Gertrude Lodge behind her. Rhoda went down the hill to meet her.

'Oh, Rhoda!' called Gertrude. 'I wanted to see you – to ask you . . .' Her face was pale and worried, and she held her left arm with her other hand. 'Somebody told me,' she said, 'about a man at Egdon Heath. They don't know his name, but they say he is a famous Wise Man, and can help people with . . . with things like this.'

She looked down at her left arm, and then looked at Rhoda, with hope in her eyes. 'They say you know about him, this Wise Man. Do you know his name?'

'Perhaps they mean Mr Trendle,' Rhoda said slowly. She felt ill. This man Trendle, people said, could do many strange things. He could understand dreams, he could drive phantoms out of houses, he could stop the work of witches . . . 'I am *not* a witch,' she thought. 'I am *not*! I do not believe in these things.'

Gertrude watched her. 'You know him,' she said. 'I can see it in your face. Of course, I don't believe in Wise Men. What can they do? But . . . well, I can just go and see him. Is it far to his house?'

'Yes – about five miles,' said Rhoda.

'Well, I must walk there. I cannot tell my husband about this. Can you come with me, Rhoda, to show me the way? Perhaps tomorrow afternoon?'

'Oh no, it's . . . I . . .' Rhoda began.

'Please!' said Gertrude.

And in the end Rhoda could not say no. Mrs Lodge was good and kind, and she needed a friend's help. But perhaps a Wise Man could see into people's dreams. Rhoda did not want to meet this man Trendle, and she was afraid . . .

���

The next afternoon she met Gertrude by the trees near her house, and they began the long walk across the hills to Egdon Heath. It was a cold day, and the sky above the hills was dark and unfriendly.

18

They began the long walk across the hills to Egdon Heath.

They found Mr Trendle's house outside the village. He was at home when they arrived. He was an old man with grey hair, and he looked long and hard at Rhoda when he saw her. Mrs Lodge told him about her arm, and he looked at it carefully.

'No, doctors can't do anything for this,' he said. 'This is the work of an enemy.'

Rhoda moved away a little.

'An enemy? What enemy?' asked Mrs Lodge.

'I don't know,' said the Wise Man, looking at her. 'But perhaps you do. I can show the person to you. Do you want me to do that?'

'Yes,' said Gertrude. 'Yes, please show me.'

Mr Trendle took Gertrude into another room, but the door was open, and Rhoda could see into the room.

The Wise Man took an egg, and did something to it. Then he put a glass of water on the table, and carefully broke the egg open. The white of the egg went down into the water, changing to a milky white colour, and moving slowly round and round.

He put the glass in front of Gertrude. 'Look down into the water,' he said. 'Look for a face.'

Gertrude stared down into the water.

'Do you see a face?' the Wise Man asked quietly.

Gertrude whispered something, but Rhoda could not hear. She turned away from the door.

'Look down into the water. Look for a face.'

When Mrs Lodge came out, her face was pale – paler than Rhoda's. Mr Trendle closed the door behind her, and the two women began to walk home. But things were not the same between them.

'Did he – did he ask for money?' Rhoda said quietly.

'Oh no, nothing. He did not want a penny,' said Gertrude.

'And what did you see?' asked Rhoda.

'Nothing . . . I – I don't want to speak about it.'

Gertrude did not look at Rhoda. Her pretty young face looked ten years older, and was now more like the face of the phantom in Rhoda's dream.

They did not speak for a long time, then Gertrude said suddenly, 'Did you *want* me to come here and see this Wise Man? How strange of you!'

'No, I didn't. But now, I am not sorry we came.'

For the first time since her dream Rhoda felt a little pleased. Life was cruel, she thought, and Gertrude Lodge must learn that lesson too.

On the long walk home they did not speak again about their visit to the Wise Man. But other people did, and whispered stories about it in all the farms and dairies. Mrs Lodge could no longer use her withered arm to do anything, and people began to put the word 'witch' in front of the name 'Rhoda Brook'.

Rhoda said nothing to anybody about the phantom of

her dream, but her face got thinner and paler. And in the spring she and her boy left their house and went away into the hills in the west.

They went away into the hills in the west.

4

The cure for a curse

Six years went past, and Mr and Mrs Lodge's married
life was not happy. The farmer said little, and did
not often smile. His wife had a withered arm, and there
were no children to call him 'father', and to run laughing
around the farmhouse. He thought of Rhoda Brook and
her son. His son. But that was the past, and he could not
change it now.

Gertrude Lodge was a different woman too. She was
only twenty-five, but she looked older. Once a happy,
smiling woman, she was now sad and worried all the
time. She loved her husband, but he no longer loved her,
and she knew it. 'Six years of married life, and only a few
months of love,' she sometimes whispered.

Her left arm was no better. She tried one thing after
another, but nothing helped it. Some of the things were a
little strange, and her husband did not like them.

'You think too much about your arm,' he said. 'You
need somebody to talk to – somebody to be around the
house. At one time there was a boy . . . I wanted him to
come and live with us, but he is too old now. And he
went away. I don't know where.'

'*You think too much about your arm,*' Farmer Lodge said.

Gertrude knew about this boy now, and all of Rhoda Brook's story, but she and her husband never spoke about it. And she never said anything to him about her visit to the Wise Man of Egdon Heath, or about the face in the glass.

She wanted so much to find a cure for her arm. 'My

husband cannot love me because of this arm,' she thought. 'So I must find a cure for it, I must. The Wise Man helped me before. Perhaps he can help me again.'

So one day she walked to Egdon Heath. She did not know the way, but at last she found the house.

'You can send away other things, I know,' she said to Trendle. 'Hair on women's faces, and things like that. Why can't you send this away?' She uncovered her poor, withered arm.

'Is there no cure, anywhere?' asked Gertrude sadly.

'No, I'm sorry, but I can't help you,' said Trendle. 'Your arm is withered because of a curse. It's not easy to find a cure for that.'

'Is there no cure, anywhere?' asked Gertrude sadly.

'There is one thing . . .' Trendle began slowly. 'But it's not easy for a woman to do.'

'Oh, tell me!' said Gertrude. 'Please!'

'You must put the withered arm on the neck of a hanged man. You must do it before he's cold – just after they take his body down.'

Gertrude's face was pale. 'How can that do good?'

'It can turn the blood, and that changes many things in the body. You must go to the jail when they hang someone, and wait for the body when they bring it in. In the old days lots of people did it; these days, not so many do it. But it is still the best cure for a curse.'

🐞 🐞 🐞

Back at home Gertrude thought about this for a long time. She tried to forget it, but she couldn't. She wanted to be pretty again, she wanted her husband to love her again. Yes, she must try this cure, she must.

'But how do I do it?' she thought. 'Where is the nearest jail? How can I get there? How often do they hang people? And when there is a hanging, how can I learn about it before it happens?'

So many questions. There was no one to help her, but

slowly she began to find the answers. She asked careful questions in the village, because country people always know everything.

One old man was very helpful. 'The nearest jail is at Casterbridge, fifteen miles away,' he told Gertrude. 'They have trials there every three months, and there's usually a hanging after the trials. Some poor man or boy takes a cow or a sheep, or just some bread, and they hang

'There's usually a hanging after the trials.'

him for it. Lots of people go to watch the hangings. I don't know why.'

The next trials were in July, Gertrude learnt. She asked her husband about them, but Lodge said very little. He was colder to her than usual, and she did not ask him again. He was often away these days, so she did not see much of him.

July came, and Gertrude went to see the helpful old man in the village again. 'Just one hanging this time,' he told her. 'It's for arson, I think. They're going to hang him next Saturday.'

Gertrude walked slowly home. 'I cannot tell my husband about this . . . this cure,' she thought. 'And how can I be away from home for two nights? What can I say to him?'

But in the end it was easy. On the Thursday before the hanging, Lodge came to her. 'I'm going away for three nights,' he said. 'It's about farm work, so you can't come with me.'

'That's all right,' Gertrude said quietly. 'I'm happy to stay at home.'

They said nothing more, and on Thursday Lodge drove away in the carriage.

5

The hangman

The next morning Gertrude got ready to leave for Casterbridge. She did not want to go by road because she did not want to meet any of her husband's friends. So she took one of the heavy horses from the farm, and rode west across the hills.

She was afraid of riding with a half-dead arm, but the farm horse was quiet and slow, and easy to ride. He carried her uphill and downhill, past rivers and through trees, moving west all the time.

The sun slowly went down in the sky, and it was nearly eight o'clock when Gertrude stopped for a moment at the top of a hill. It was the last hill before the town, and she could see the roofs of Casterbridge below. There was a big building on a hill at the end of the town, with a white roof. She knew this was the jail, and she could see a lot of workmen on the roof.

'What are they doing?' she thought. 'They're building something up there on the roof . . . Oh!'

Suddenly, she understood, and quickly turned her eyes away. It was a warm summer evening, but she shivered with cold.

Gertrude could see the roofs of Casterbridge below.

'Tomorrow they're going to hang a man on that roof,' she thought. 'And when he is dead . . .'

She shivered again, but then she remembered her husband's cold words and his unsmiling face, and she rode on down into the town.

31

She found a room to stay for the night, and then went out into the town.

'What do I do now?' she thought. 'How can I get into the jail tomorrow? Who must I talk to? The men at the jail, or the hangman?'

'Who are you?' the man called out. 'What do you want?'

She was afraid to go to the jail, so she went to find the hangman. He had a house down by the river, a boy in the town told her.

When she found the house, she stood outside for some minutes, afraid to go to the door. Then the door opened and a man came out.

'Who are you?' he called out. 'What do you want?'

'I want to speak to you for a minute.'

He came nearer, and looked at her. 'Well, well, that's a pretty face,' he said. 'Come into the house.'

They went inside. Davies (that was his name) was a hangman on some days, but a gardener on other days.

'Is it about gardening work?' he asked Gertrude. 'I can't do any tomorrow, because I'm working at the jail.'

'Yes, yes, I know. That's why I'm here.'

'Ah! I thought so. Is the poor man one of your family then? Perhaps your young brother? No,' – Davies looked at Gertrude's dress – 'I don't think so. Was he one of your farm workers perhaps?'

'No. What time is the hanging?'

'The same as usual – twelve o'clock.'

'And it is . . . it *is* going to happen, yes?'

'Oh yes, nothing can stop the hanging now,' said Davies. 'But I'm sorry for this young man, I truly am. He's only eighteen. They say it was arson, but I don't know. He was there when the fire began, but there were twenty other men there too. So how do they know? I think they just want to hang someone . . . anyone. But what can I do for you, my pretty?'

'I need a cure,' Gertrude said, 'a cure for a curse. And a Wise Man told me about the hanged man, and – and turning the blood . . .'

'Oh yes, miss! Now I understand. People sometimes come for that. But not pretty young things like you. Well, well. What's the cure for?'

'It's this.' Gertrude uncovered her left arm.

'Ah! It's all withered,' said the hangman, looking at it.

'Yes,' she said.

'Well, a hanged man's neck is the best cure for that,' he said. 'Your Wise Man was right.'

'So can you help me?' Gertrude whispered.

'Usually people go to the jail, and take their doctor with them, and give their name and address . . . But yes, I can help you – for a little money, perhaps.'

'Oh, thank you!' Gertrude said. 'It's better like this. I don't want people to know about it.'

'Don't want your lover to know, eh?'

'No – husband.'

'Aha! Very well. You can touch the body.'

'Where is it now?' she said, shivering.

'It? – *He*, you mean; he's still alive tonight. He's in the jail, a little room right at the top.'

'And what must I do tomorrow?' Gertrude said.

'There's a little door at the back of the jail. Be there at one o'clock, no later. I can open the door from inside, and can take you to the body when they bring him in. Goodnight. Don't be late. And you don't want people to see you, so cover your face. Goodnight, my pretty!'

Gertrude went away, and walked up to the jail on the hill. She wanted to find the little door at the back, to know it for tomorrow. Then she went back down into the town and went to her room, and waited for the morning.

'There's a little door at the back of the jail.'

6

The blood turns

At half past twelve on Saturday Gertrude Lodge walked up the hill to the jail. She went there by the small back streets, because there were so many people in the town. They were there for a holiday, to watch the hanging.

At one o'clock she was inside the jail. The hangman took her to a long dark room with a table. 'Wait there,' he told her. 'Two or three minutes, no more.'

Four men came into the room with a long box.

He went away, and Gertrude waited. She had a veil over her face, and her left arm was uncovered, ready. She stood still, with her eyes closed, listening, and shivering with terror.

Soon she heard noises, and could hear heavy feet on the stairs. The heavy feet came nearer, and four men came into the room with a long box. It was open, and in it was the body of a young man, with a cover over his face. The men put the box down on the table.

'Now!' said a voice in Gertrude's ear. 'Now!'

But the young woman was half-dead with terror, and at first she could not move. Then she opened her eyes and came up to the table. She could hear other noises outside the room. There were more people coming.

Davies the hangman was by her side. He uncovered the body's face, took Gertrude's hand, and put her arm across the dead man's neck.

Gertrude screamed.

And at once there was a second scream. A woman's scream, but not Gertrude's. Gertrude turned round.

Behind her stood Rhoda Brook, her face pale, and her eyes red with crying. Behind Rhoda stood Gertrude's husband. He looked old and sad, but there were no tears in his eyes.

'You! What in God's name are *you* doing here?' he whispered angrily.

'Oh, cruel, cruel woman!' cried Rhoda. 'Why do you come between us and our child now? This is the true meaning of my dream! You are like that cruel phantom at last!'

When Gertrude saw her husband with Rhoda, she knew at once that the dead young man was Rhoda's son. She stared at Rhoda, with terror in her eyes.

Then Rhoda ran to Gertrude, closed her hand round the younger woman's arm, and pulled her away from the table. When she let go of the arm, the young wife fell down, at her husband's feet.

She never opened her eyes again. They carried her out of the jail into the town, but she never got home alive. Perhaps it was the 'turning of the blood', perhaps it was her withered arm, perhaps it was her terror in the jail when she turned and saw Rhoda behind her. Doctors came and looked at her, but they could do nothing to help her, and three days later she died.

🕸 🕸 🕸

In those days the unhappy parents of a hanged man came and took the body away after the hanging. That was why Farmer Lodge was at the jail with Rhoda that day. It was not his first visit to the jail. With Rhoda, he went many times to visit his son that summer, and that was why he was away from the farm so often.

But after his young wife died, nobody ever saw

Rhoda ran to Gertrude, and pulled her away from the table.

Farmer Lodge in Casterbridge again. He went home to his farm, but he did not stay there long. After a short time he sold the farm and the farmhouse, and all the cows and sheep and horses. Then he went away to live in a small town by the sea. He lived very quietly, without any friends or family near him.

When he died two years later, he left a lot of money. Most of it went to a home for poor boys, but there was money for Rhoda Brook too.

For some time nobody could find Rhoda. Then one day she came back to her old house near the dairy. But she never took a penny of Farmer Lodge's money. She went back to work in the dairy, and worked there for many long years, milking the cows in the morning, and again in the evening. Her dark hair turned white, and her sad pale face looked thin and old.

Most people knew Rhoda's story, and sometimes they watched her at milking time. What did she think about, all those long days, at morning and evening milking?

But nobody ever asked her, and nobody ever knew the answer.

GLOSSARY

arson the crime of setting fire to a building
believe to think that something is true or real
blood the red liquid inside the body
carriage a kind of 'car' that is pulled by horses
cow a farm animal that gives milk
cruel not kind; giving pain or unhappiness to other people
cure *(n)* something to make an illness go away
curse *(n)* asking for something bad to happen to someone
dairy a place where cows are milked, milk is kept, etc.
dream *(n)* a picture in your head when you are sleeping
egg a round thing laid by a chicken, which we eat
enemy a person who hates you; the opposite of 'friend'
fall (past tense **fell**) to go down quickly; to drop
farmer a person who owns a farm (a place to keep animals and
    grow food)
flesh the soft part of your body under the skin
God (dear God) words you say when you are surprised or
    afraid
hang to kill somebody by holding them above the ground by a
    rope around the neck
hangman a person whose job is to hang criminals
heavy difficult to move or carry
horse an animal that you can ride, or that can pull carriages
innocent an innocent person has done nothing bad or wrong
jail a prison
kind friendly and helpful
mark *(n)* if you touch a piece of paper with a wet, dirty finger,
    you leave a mark on the paper

married having a husband or a wife
milkmaid a woman who works in a dairy, milking cows
pale with no colour in the face
phantom a ghost; a 'person' who is not real
poor with very little money; also, a word you use when you feel
    sorry for someone or something
pretty nice to look at
ride *(v)* to sit on a horse's back when it moves
sad not happy
scream *(v)* to make a loud high cry when you are afraid or hurt
shiver *(v)* to shake with cold, or fear
stare *(v)* to look at something for a long time
strange very unusual or surprising
sweet kind and gentle
tears water that comes from the eyes when you cry
terror very great fear
thin not fat
trial a time when a judge decides if a criminal has done
    something wrong or not
uncover to take something from the top of another thing
veil a piece of material that a woman puts over her head and
    face
wedding-ring a ring on the third finger, to show you are married
whisper to speak very, very quietly
wise knowing and understanding many things
witch a woman who can make bad things happen to people
withered thin and weak, looking old and dry and dead
worried afraid that something bad is going to happen

The Withered Arm

ACTIVITIES

Before Reading

1 Read the story introduction on the first page of the book, and the back cover. What do you know now about the story? Tick one box for each sentence.

	YES	NO
1 Farmer Lodge marries his first love.	☐	☐
2 Farmer Lodge is married.	☐	☐
3 Only one of the women works.	☐	☐
4 One of the women has a child.	☐	☐
5 The arm is withered because of an accident.	☐	☐
6 The withered arm gets worse and worse.	☐	☐
7 The withered arm has the marks of teeth on it.	☐	☐

2 What can you guess about the people in this story? Use this table to make some sentences.

		a withered arm.
Rhoda		the wife.
Gertrude	is	the mother.
The boy	has	a witch.
Mr Lodge		a son.
		a short life.
		a long life.

While Reading

Read Chapters 1 and 2, then circle the correct words in each sentence.

1 The farmer's new wife was *Gertrude / Rhoda.*
2 The boy lived with his *mother / father.*
3 The boy met Farmer Lodge and his wife *at the farm / on the road / at his house.*
4 Rhoda was *younger / older* and *taller / shorter* than Gertrude.
5 In her dream Rhoda saw a phantom of *Farmer Lodge / Gertrude.*
6 Rhoda met Gertrude *before / after* the dream.
7 To Rhoda, Gertrude looked like *a friend / an enemy.*
8 On Gertrude's *right / left* arm, there were marks made by *teeth / fingers.*

How do you feel about the people in the story? Put a circle round one answer for each person.

Do you feel sorry for . . .
1 Rhoda?   yes / a little / no
2 the boy?   yes / a little / no
3 Gertrude?   yes / a little / no
4 Mr Lodge?   yes / a little / no

Before you read Chapter 3, can you guess what happens? Choose some of these answers.

1 Gertrude's arm does not get better.

2 Farmer Lodge calls Rhoda a witch.

3 Farmer Lodge begins to love Gertrude less.

4 Farmer Lodge leaves his wife.

5 Gertrude asks Rhoda for help.

6 Gertrude sees the face of her enemy.

7 Rhoda tells Gertrude about her dream.

8 Rhoda's son goes to live with his father and Gertrude.

9 Rhoda and her son leave their house and go away.

Read Chapters 3 and 4, then put these sentences in the correct order for the story. Begin with number 5.

1 Gertrude asked the country people about hanging.

2 Things were different between Gertrude and Rhoda.

3 Gertrude went to see Mr Trendle again.

4 Farmer Lodge went away for three nights.

5 Rhoda and Gertrude went to see Mr Trendle.

6 People began to call Rhoda a witch.

7 Gertrude learnt about a hanging in July in Casterbridge.

8 Rhoda left her house and went away.

9 Gertrude saw a face in the glass.

10 Six years went by and Gertrude's arm was still withered.

11 Mr Trendle told Gertrude about the best cure for a curse.

Before you read Chapter 5, can you guess what happens? Choose one ending for each sentence.

1 Gertrude . . .

    a) meets one of her husband's friends on the road.

    b) meets Farmer Lodge in Casterbridge.

    c) meets the hangman in Casterbridge.

2 Mr Lodge . . .

    a) returns home the next day before Gertrude leaves.

    b) goes away to meet Rhoda Brook somewhere.

    c) stops Gertrude going to Casterbridge.

Read Chapter 5. You are Gertrude's friend. What do you say to her about tomorrow? Choose one idea.

1 'Go to the jail.'   3 'Go home.'

2 'Don't go to the jail.'   4 'Go to church.'

Before you read Chapter 6, look at these ideas. Can you guess how many are true? Choose as many as you like.

After Gertrude puts her arm on the hanged man's neck . . .

1 . . . the hangman asks her for a lot more money.

2 . . . she sees the hanged man's mother behind her.

3 . . . her withered arm gets better at once.

4 . . . her hair turns white.

5 . . . she dies three days later.

6 . . . she goes home and lives happily with her husband.

After Reading

1 **Use the clues below to complete this crossword with words from the story. Then find the hidden seven-letter word in the crossword.**

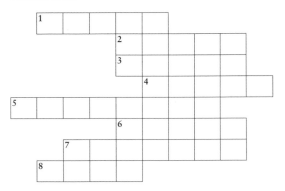

1 Perhaps a _____ put her hand on Gertrude's arm.

2 Rhoda worked in a _____, milking the cows.

3 Rhoda thought, 'Gertrude is a friend, not an _____.'

4 Mr Trendle put water and the white of an egg in a _____.

5 When Rhoda saw Gertrude at the jail, she _____.

6 On Gertrude's arm there were some yellowy-brown

_____.

7 In Rhoda's dream a _____ sat on her body.

8 Gertrude hoped to find a _____ for her arm at the jail.

The hidden word in the crossword is _____ .

2 Farmer Lodge and Gertrude never talked about Rhoda and her son – but imagine that they did. Here are five questions for Gertrude to ask, and ten answers for Mr Lodge. Match two answers to each question.

1 Why didn't you marry Rhoda?
2 Why did you stop loving her?
3 Why did she stay when I came?
4 Why didn't you help your son?
5 Why didn't you tell me about her?

6 Because she did not have much money, and she had work and a house here.
7 Because she was only a milkmaid.
8 Because it was a long time ago, and it wasn't important.
9 Because I was young, and young love soon dies.
10 Because his mother didn't want my money.
11 Because I wanted my wife to be rich and from a good family.
12 Because I wanted you to be happy.
13 Because I wanted somebody new.
14 Because she was interested in my new wife.
15 Because he had food, and a place to live, so I didn't think about him.

Now look at the two answers for each question. Choose the best answer for Farmer Lodge to make, and explain why you think that answer is best.

3 Here is a new illustration for the story. Find the best place in the story to put the picture, and answer these questions.

The picture goes on page _____.

1 Who are the two people in the picture?
2 What are they talking about?
3 What does the woman do the next day?

Now write a caption for the illustration.

Caption: _____

4 Here are two different endings for the story. Use these words to fill in the gaps.

better, die, dies, dream, fingers, happy, many, marries, phantom, sees, together

1 Gertrude does not _____ and her arm gets _____. She and Mr Lodge live _____ for many years and they have _____ children. Nobody ever _____ Rhoda again.

2 After Gertrude _____, Mr Lodge _____ Rhoda, but they are not _____. One night Rhoda has another _____ about a _____, and the next day Mr Lodge sees the marks of _____ on his arm . . .

Which ending do you like best – the ending of the story in the book, or one of the endings above? Why?

5 How did you feel about the people in this story? Use these names, and complete the sentences in your own words.

Rhoda / Gertrude / the boy / Mr Lodge
1 I felt most sorry for _____ because _____.
2 I did not feel sorry for _____ because _____.
3 I also felt sorry for _____ because _____.

6 Some people believe that there are things like phantoms and witches and wise men. Why is that, do you think? Do *you* believe in them?

ABOUT THE AUTHOR

Thomas Hardy (1840–1928) was born in the village of Higher Bockhampton in Dorset, in the south of England. At twenty-two he went to London to work as an architect, and there he started writing poems and stories and novels.

His fourth novel, *Far from the Madding Crowd* (1874), was very popular, and from this he earned enough money to stop working and also to get married. Other successful novels followed, but when *Tess of the d'Urbervilles* and *Jude the Obscure* were published, readers did not like them at all, saying they were dark and cruel. After this, Hardy stopped writing novels and returned to poetry.

For most of his life he lived in Dorset with his first wife Emma, and soon after she died he married again. After his death his heart was buried in Emma's grave.

When he was a young man, Hardy loved listening to old people telling stories of country life. Were the stories true? Hardy once described one of the old musicians from his village as 'a man who speaks neither truth or lies, but something halfway between the two which is very enjoyable'.

Hardy used many of these old stories in his own writing, and this was also true for *The Withered Arm*. He said that when he was a boy, there was a very old woman in his village, who told stories about witches and wise men and strange dark dreams. In those days many people believed in things like that. Were there ever two women called Rhoda and Gertrude? Nobody knows, but many people think that *The Withered Arm* is one of Hardy's best stories.

OXFORD BOOKWORMS LIBRARY

Classics • Crime & Mystery • Factfiles • Fantasy & Horror
Human Interest • Playscripts • Thriller & Adventure
True Stories • World Stories

The OXFORD BOOKWORMS LIBRARY provides enjoyable reading in English, with a wide range of classic and modern fiction, non-fiction, and plays. It includes original and adapted texts in seven carefully graded language stages, which take learners from beginner to advanced level. An overview is given on the next pages.

All Stage 1 titles are available as audio recordings, as well as over eighty other titles from Starter to Stage 6. All Starters and many titles at Stages 1 to 4 are specially recommended for younger learners. Every Bookworm is illustrated, and Starters and Factfiles have full-colour illustrations.

The OXFORD BOOKWORMS LIBRARY also offers extensive support. Each book contains an introduction to the story, notes about the author, a glossary, and activities. Additional resources include tests and worksheets, and answers for these and for the activities in the books. There is advice on running a class library, using audio recordings, and the many ways of using Oxford Bookworms in reading programmes. Resource materials are available on the website <www.oup.com/elt/bookworms>.

The *Oxford Bookworms Collection* is a series for advanced learners. It consists of volumes of short stories by well-known authors, both classic and modern. Texts are not abridged or adapted in any way, but carefully selected to be accessible to the advanced student.

You can find details and a full list of titles in the *Oxford Bookworms Library Catalogue* and *Oxford English Language Teaching Catalogues,* and on the website <www.oup.com/elt/bookworms>.

THE OXFORD BOOKWORMS LIBRARY
GRADING AND SAMPLE EXTRACTS

STARTER • 250 HEADWORDS

present simple – present continuous – imperative –
can/cannot, must – *going to* (future) – simple gerunds …

Her phone is ringing – but where is it?

Sally gets out of bed and looks in her bag. No phone. She looks under the bed. No phone. Then she looks behind the door. There is her phone. Sally picks up her phone and answers it. *Sally's Phone*

STAGE 1 • 400 HEADWORDS

… past simple – coordination with *and, but, or* –
subordination with *before, after, when, because, so* …

I knew him in Persia. He was a famous builder and I worked with him there. For a time I was his friend, but not for long. When he came to Paris, I came after him – I wanted to watch him. He was a very clever, very dangerous man. *The Phantom of the Opera*

STAGE 2 • 700 HEADWORDS

… present perfect – *will* (future) – *(don't) have to, must not, could* –
comparison of adjectives – simple *if* clauses – past continuous –
tag questions – *ask/tell* + infinitive …

While I was writing these words in my diary, I decided what to do. I must try to escape. I shall try to get down the wall outside. The window is high above the ground, but I have to try. I shall take some of the gold with me – if I escape, perhaps it will be helpful later. *Dracula*

... should, may – present perfect continuous – *used to* – past perfect –
causative – relative clauses – indirect statements ...

Of course, it was most important that no one should see
Colin, Mary, or Dickon entering the secret garden. So Colin
gave orders to the gardeners that they must all keep away
from that part of the garden in future. *The Secret Garden*

STAGE 4 • 1400 HEADWORDS

... past perfect continuous – passive (simple forms) –
would conditional clauses – indirect questions –
relatives with *where/when* – gerunds after prepositions/phrases ...

I was glad. Now Hyde could not show his face to the world
again. If he did, every honest man in London would be proud
to report him to the police. *Dr Jekyll and Mr Hyde*

STAGE 5 • 1800 HEADWORDS

... future continuous – future perfect –
passive (modals, continuous forms) –
would have conditional clauses – modals + perfect infinitive ...

If he had spoken Estella's name, I would have hit him. I was so
angry with him, and so depressed about my future, that I could
not eat the breakfast. Instead I went straight to the old house.
Great Expectations

STAGE 6 • 2500 HEADWORDS

... passive (infinitives, gerunds) – advanced modal meanings –
clauses of concession, condition

When I stepped up to the piano, I was confident. It was as if I
knew that the prodigy side of me really did exist. And when I
started to play, I was so caught up in how lovely I looked that
I didn't worry how I would sound. *The Joy Luck Club*

The Phantom of the Opera

JENNIFER BASSETT

It is 1880, in the Opera House in Paris. Everybody is talking about the Phantom of the Opera, the ghost that lives somewhere under the Opera House. The Phantom is a man in black clothes. He is a body without a head, he is a head without a body. He has a yellow face, he has no nose, he has black holes for eyes. Everybody is afraid of the Phantom – the singers, the dancers, the directors, the Stage workers . . .

But who has actually seen him?

Pocahontas

RETOLD BY TIM VICARY

A beautiful young Indian girl, and a brave Englishman. Black eyes, and blue eyes. A friendly smile, a laugh, a look of love . . . But this is North America in 1607, and love is not easy. The girl is the daughter of King Powhatan, and the Englishman is a white man. And the Indians of Virginia do not want the white men in their beautiful country.

This is the famous story of Pocahontas, and her love for the Englishman John Smith.